A TRUE BOOK™

W9-AYB-947

Animal Camouflage

VICKY FRANCHINO

Children's Press®
An Imprint of Scholastic Inc.

Content Consultant
Dr. Stephen S. Ditchkoff
Professor of Wildlife Sciences
Auburn University
Auburn, Alabama

Library of Congress Cataloging-in-Publication Data
Franchino, Vicky, author.
 Animal camouflage / by Vicky Franchino.
   pages cm. — (A true book)
 Summary: "Learn all about animals that rely on camouflage to help them stay hidden, whether
it's to avoid predators or launch a surprise attack on prey" — Provided by publisher.
 Includes bibliographical references and index.
 ISBN 978-0-531-21548-7 (library binding) — ISBN 978-0-531-21585-2 (pbk.)
 1. Camouflage (Biology)—Juvenile literature. I. Title. II. Series: True book.
 QH546.F69 2016
 591.47'2—dc23   2015003979

© 2016 Scholastic Inc.
All rights reserved. Published in 2016 by Children's Press, an imprint of Scholastic Inc. Published
simultaneously in Canada. Printed in the United States of America 40
SCHOLASTIC, CHILDREN'S PRESS, A TRUE BOOK™, and associated logos are trademarks and/or
registered trademarks of Scholastic Inc.
8 9 10 11 12 13 14 15 16 17 R 28 27 26 25 24 23 22 21 20 19

Front cover: A saturniid moth on leaf litter in Shaanxi, China

Back cover: A leaf-tailed gecko on a tree trunk in Madagascar

Find the Truth!

Everything you are about to read is true *except* for one of the sentences on this page.

Which one is **TRUE**?

T or F Sea horses look for coral that is the same color as they are.

T or F Chameleons use color to show their temperature and mood.

Find the answers in this book.

Contents

THE **BIG** TRUTH!

Humans and Camouflage

3 Hiding Underwater

Zebras

4 A Good Match

How do zebras' stripes work as camouflage? **35**

Many parrot species have brightly colored feathers.

5

CHAPTER 1

Masters of Disguise

A hungry damselfish swims through the ocean. As it searches for lunch, it is startled to see a banded sea snake directly ahead. To avoid becoming this animal's next meal, the damselfish turns and swims away quickly. But wait! Was that really a sea snake? No! It was a **mimic** octopus using a clever disguise. The damselfish would have attacked the creature instead of swimming away. This octopus protects itself by changing its color, texture, and shape.

The mimic octopus knows which is the best animal to copy to scare off a predator.

What Is Camouflage?

If you walked quietly into a forest, you might think there were very few animals to be found. But wait a few minutes and look carefully. Do you see animals that are using their color and texture to blend into their surroundings? This is known as **camouflage**. Some creatures use camouflage to avoid being eaten. Others use it to hide from their prey.

Both the color and shape of this emerald moth's wings help it blend in with its surroundings.

The coloring of the hoverfly (right) mimics the stripes of the honeybee (left).

What Is Mimicry?

Mimicry means a creature appears to be something it is not. The harmless hoverfly has black and yellow stripes like a bee. Would-be predators stay far away so they won't be stung! Because birds do not always know if a butterfly is a viceroy (harmless, but nasty tasting) or a monarch (poisonous), they avoid both. Sometimes, an animal will actually change itself to stay out of trouble. The mimic octopus is an example of this.

Flounders and other flatfish model themselves after the sandy ocean floor.

Model Behavior

When an animal uses camouflage, it finds something to copy or model itself after. Some creatures will copy a color, while others will copy a texture or an action. It is very common for an animal to model a background such as grass, leaves, or tree bark, and then hide in plain sight!

Cryptic Coloration

At first glance, a section of tree bark might look like plain old bark. But look closer. There, in the swirls and textures of the rough bark, you might find many kinds of creatures. The **cryptic** coloration of moths, crickets, grasshoppers, and other insects makes them look just like the bark. This lets these animals vanish within their surroundings.

A hawk moth hides against the bark of a tree in Thailand.

Sticking Around

While some creatures rely on color or texture to blend into the background, others pretend to be another object or organism. Stick insects camouflage themselves by looking just like a stick. These insects are shades of gray, brown, or green. They are very good at sitting completely still. Sometimes they sit for hours, just like a stick would!

Most stick insects stay still in the day and hunt at night.

12

The broad-headed bug nymph lives among the ants it mimics.

Acting the Part

The broad-headed bug **nymph** not only *looks* like an ant, it acts like one. Predators see its rapid antennae movements and zigzag walk and think it must be part of a large—and dangerous—ant colony. A snake called the death adder uses mimicry not to drive animals away, but to tempt them closer. Its tail looks and moves like a tasty caterpillar. But when a hungry lizard goes in for a bite, it ends up as the meal!

Bird-dropping spiders mimic both the look and smell of bird feces.

Ick!

Some **species** stay out of trouble by pretending to be something that every creature avoids. The bird-dropping spider is a great example. This spider looks just like a large mound of bird dung! Some birds and bigger insects might have found this spider to be a tasty treat. But they take one look and decide to avoid it. Scientists have even done research that proved this was true.

Moody Lizards

Quick! Name a creature that changes color. Did you say "chameleon"? This lizard is known for changing color, but chameleons don't do it to hide. They use color to control their body temperature or show what kind of mood they are in. The chameleon's outer skin is **transparent**. Underneath it are layers that hold special cells called chromatophores. These cells can grow or shrink, which makes the chameleon appear to be different colors.

Hide and Seek

Grasshoppers are a favorite treat for many creatures. Everything from lizards, snakes, and toads to rats, gophers, and coyotes enjoy a delicious grasshopper dinner. But grasshoppers have a good trick to avoid being eaten: camouflage. Stone grasshoppers in Australia and Africa come in shades of brown, gray, and white. This helps them vanish next to sand and rock. Green and brown grasshoppers can disappear in leaves and underbrush.

 The long-headed grasshopper has the shape and colors of the grass it lives among.

The Grasshopper's Cousin

If you placed a katydid next to a grasshopper, you would probably have a hard time telling them apart. They are related to each other and look very similar. But these insects have something besides their looks in common. They are both experts at disappearing! Like grasshoppers, adult katydids usually protect themselves by blending in. Katydid nymphs take a different approach. They mimic dangerous insects to avoid being eaten.

Katydids may be a variety of colors, depending on the types of plants in their habitat.

Praying mantises remain much the same shape and coloring from the time they hatch.

Shape and Color

Some animals rely on their coloring for camouflage. The praying mantis goes a step further and also uses its shape. With its flat, triangular body, this insect finds it easy to disguise itself against the flat, triangular leaves it hides on. The praying mantis is usually green if it lives in wet areas. It might be more brown or gray if its home area is dry.

A change in the environment has caused lighter peppered moths (left) to blend into trees better than darker peppered moths (right).

Changing With the Times

Some species change their camouflage over time. One famous example is the peppered moth of Britain. This moth was once white with small black specks. It could easily blend in against light-colored trees. As pollution darkened the tree bark, an interesting thing happened: The moths became darker, too. They gradually changed to match their surroundings. Today, there is less air pollution in Britain. The trees—and the peppered moth—are turning white once again.

Find the Cricket

Crickets are found on every continent except Antarctica. It is easy to tell where a cricket lives based on its coloring and body shape. Black and brown crickets are found on the ground or in piles of decaying leaves. Green crickets hide on fresh leaves or in bushes or gardens. Some crickets have an extra advantage: a leaf-shaped body that makes it even easier to hide.

Male crickets chirp by rubbing their wings together. Female crickets do not chirp.

The Time of Their Life

Many species are different colors depending on the stage in their life cycle. Looper moth caterpillars are a brownish color. To hide, they attach their body to a branch and then hold still. They look just like twigs, so their predators do not bother them. When they change into moths, the loopers are a patterned, grayish color. In this stage, they are almost invisible against the tree bark where they live.

A looper moth caterpillar sticks out from a pine tree, like a branch.

Owl butterflies are common in the forests of Central and South America.

Protection

A hungry lizard searches for food. As it scampers over branches, it sees a large, owl-like eye staring right at it! Startled, the lizard runs away. It does not know that this "eye" belongs to an owl butterfly, not an owl. The owl butterfly uses its "eyes" to scare an attacker away. It also uses them to trick other animals to attack a less sensitive part of its body. This is called **deflection**.

Humans and Camouflage

A deer walks through the forest. It waits and watches, trying to see if there is an animal waiting to attack. It does not notice the human hunter wearing a suit and hat made of camouflage material.

Humans typically use camouflage for hunting and in war. They do not use it just for clothing. Tanks and airplanes have been covered in "camo," too.

Human camouflage is usually a combination of colors and patterns. The choice of color depends on the area where the camouflage will be used. In a desert setting, tan camouflage is common. In a forest, camouflage might be green and brown. White camouflage has been used to hide people and vehicles against a snowy background.

The pattern of the camouflage is important, too. It acts as a type of disruptive coloration. It is used to hide where a person's body or a vehicle begins or ends.

CHAPTER 3

Hiding Underwater

Coral reefs are home to an amazing variety of ocean creatures. One is the pygmy sea horse. This species' skin is covered with tiny bumps called tubercles and is exactly the color of the coral that hides it. Pygmy sea horses come in many different colors. Do they have to find coral that matches their skin color? No! Sea horses can change to become the color of their coral host!

 Pygmy sea horses have curly tails they use to hold on to coral reefs when they are hiding.

Flounders have to hide from both sea creatures and birds.

The Eyes Have It

The flounder has a flat shape and coloring that matches the ocean floor. These are typical tools for camouflage. But this fish also has something unique: special eyes. At birth, its eyes are positioned one on either side of its flat body. As it gets older, both eyes move to one side of its body. The flounder can now swim on its side, making it look flatter and more difficult for predators to see. And when it hides on its side in the sand, both eyes can be on the lookout.

In the Clear

Jellyfish have two features that help them hide from predators and sneak up on their prey. One is their color. Deep-sea jellyfish come in very dark colors that let them disappear in the murky world of the ocean. The other feature is their transparency. With a body that is 95 percent water, jellyfish are basically see-through. It is easy for them to hide just by staying still!

Jellyfish have existed for more than 500 million years.

Dragon of the Deep

Dragons are usually fierce creatures in fairy tales. However, the sea dragon is quite delicate and fragile. This species lives in the oceans of Australia. It is related to the sea horse. A sea dragon's entire body is covered with long, floating "arms" that look just like the seaweed it likes to hide among. Although it has fins for steering, the sea dragon usually simply floats. This makes it look even more like seaweed!

Sea dragons are quite rare and close to being endangered.

Cuttlefish might change color to communicate.

Camouflage King

Cuttlefish don't change just their color, texture, *or* shape—they can change all three! Like the chameleon, they have chromatophores. The cuttlefish expand and contract muscles around these special cells. This changes the color, texture, and shape of their bodies. Often they sneak up on prey through camouflage. Sometimes they put on a colorful show that dazzles and slows down the prey instead!

Some decorator crabs alter their appearance using stinging anemones.

Exterior Decorating

Did you just see a plant walk by? It might have been a decorator crab. This creature hides by attaching small plants and animals to its shell. The shell is covered with setae, which are tiny hooks. They hold on to the "decorations" that camouflage the crab. This crab will grow throughout its life. It periodically sheds its old shell and grows a new, bigger one. But this thrifty crab reuses the decorations from its old shell.

Fooled You

To survive, some species take advantage of the good reputation of another species. The false cleaner fish (below, left) is an example. It looks a lot like the striped cleaner wrasse (below, right), which eats **parasites** off other fish. Fish that want to be cleaned of their parasites sometimes swim up to the false cleaner fish, mistaking it for the striped cleaner wrasse. But they are in for a surprise. Instead of having their parasites eaten, these fish will probably have big bites taken out of them!

CHAPTER 4

A Good Match

The world is filled with examples of small animals' camouflage and mimicry. But larger animals use these abilities, too. It might seem like animals that live in forests, deserts, and plains would need to camouflage themselves with dull colors. The owl is a good example of this. But many animals use very bright colors as camouflage. Think of the parrot in the jungle. A parrot's bright colors confuse a predator's eyes, making the bird difficult to see.

Some parrots use their bright colors to warn enemies away from their nests.

Seeing Is Not Everything

How do animals match their color to their surroundings? It might seem logical to assume they use their sight. But researchers have found that the Moorish gecko probably uses something else: its skin's sense of touch! When this gecko was blindfolded, it could still change color to match its surroundings. But when its body was wrapped, it could not! Cells in its skin help this gecko know which color to turn.

The Moorish gecko can make its skin darker or lighter.

Can you spot the dragon lizard among the rocks?

Almost Invisible

Dragon lizards are a popular food for a variety of animals. However, these lizards have a way of protecting themselves from predators. If they realize they are in danger, they freeze and seem to vanish against the background. Dragon lizards come in a number of colors and live in many places throughout Australia. Some are reddish brown and live in the desert, where they hide among rocks. Others are dull gray and live near water or trees.

A fawn's spots vanish in its first year of life.

Hidden in the Forest

A newborn fawn is no match for the bears, coyotes, and bobcats that might enjoy making a meal of it. But the colors of the fur on the fragile fawn protect it from being seen. The white spots on its brown fur look like sunlight against the forest floor. The mother deer counts on this protection when she leaves the baby alone and goes to search for food.

Seasonal Camouflage

During the long months of winter, the Arctic landscape is a sea of white. But when summer comes, it changes to gray and brown. To survive in this shifting land, many animals change their color by molting. This means they lose a coat of feathers or fur and grow a new one. The arctic fox, arctic hare, and ptarmigan all have a winter coat that matches the winter landscapes and a summer one that matches their summer surroundings.

Camouflaged by its white winter coat, the arctic fox is able to hunt down prey undetected.

Blending In by Standing Out

Imagine a herd of zebras standing together. Now, imagine trying to figure out where one zebra starts and another one ends. It is very hard to do! That is the idea behind disruptive coloration. With this form of camouflage, an animal's pattern of stripes or spots hides it. A predator will have a hard time picking out one animal to attack among the herd.

A herd of zebras can hide their numbers by standing together.

When viewed from the side, this shark's countershading becomes more obvious, with its dark top and light underbelly.

Predators Hide, Too

Animals of prey are not the only ones to use camouflage. Predators do, too! Just as a zebra uses its stripes to confuse a lion, a leopard uses its spots to hide from a creature it is stalking. **Countershading** helps a shark disappear. When viewed from the top, its body is dark and looks like the water below. When viewed from below, its white underbelly looks like the sky above.

Sloths rely on algae for food as well as for camouflage.

Slow Moving

Some animals can rely on speed to escape an animal that is chasing them, but not the sloth. This animal moves very slowly—only about 6 feet (2 meters) in a minute. In fact, it moves so slowly that fungi and algae have a chance to grow on its fur! But these clever creatures put these plants to good use. They feed them to their children, and they rely on their greenish tint for camouflage.

Skin of Many Colors

Frogs come in various colors that have different uses. Some frogs are leaf-green, dull brown, or gray to hide in their surroundings. Others, like the poison dart frog, have brightly colored skin that signals, "Keep away! I'm poisonous!" But this warning is not always true. Some nonpoisonous frogs look just like their poisonous relatives to trick predators into staying away from them.

Camouflage is just one of the many ways animals protect themselves. Every species does it a little differently, and there is a lot more to learn about how animals trick one another! ★

Poison dart frogs produce some of the world's most powerful toxins.

Number of animals a mimic octopus can copy: More than 10

Number of chromatophores a cuttlefish has: 200 per 0.002 sq. in. (1 sq mm) of skin

Size of a pygmy sea horse: 0.8 in. (2 cm), about the size of a paper clip

Percentage of a jellyfish's body that is made up of water: 95

Percentage of a human body that is made up of water: 65

Number of species of cuttlefish: More than 100

Number of species of frogs: More than 4,000

Number of layers of skin a chameleon has: Four, from outer to inner layer: the epidermis, the chromatophore layer, the melanophore layer, and the nether layer

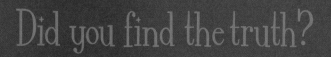

Did you find the truth?

F Sea horses look for coral that is the same color as they are.

T Chameleons use color to show their temperature and mood.

Resources

Books

Pryor, Kimberley Jane. *Mimicry and Relationships*. New York: Marshall Cavendish Benchmark, 2010.

Racanelli, Marie. *Camouflaged Creatures*. New York: PowerKids Press, 2010.

Zborowski, Paul. *Can You Find Me? Nature's Hidden Creatures*. Sydney: Young Reed, 2010.

Visit this Scholastic Web site for more information on animal camouflage:
⭐ www.factsfornow.scholastic.com
Enter the keywords **Animal Camouflage**

Important Words

camouflage (KAM-uh-flahzh) — a disguise or a natural coloring that allows animals, people, or objects to hide by making them look like their surroundings

countershading (KOUN-tur-shay-ding) — protective coloring of some animals where they are darker on the upper side and lighter on the underside

cryptic (KRIP-tik) — not clear; serving to conceal

deflection (di-FLEKT-shun) —the act of making something go a different direction

disruptive coloration (dis-RUHP-tive kuhl-ur-AY-shun) — a form of camouflage that uses a contrasting pattern to make it hard to see the outline of an animal or object

mimic (MIM-ik) — imitates someone or something else

nymph (NIMF) — a young form of an insect

parasites (PAR-uh-sites) — animals or plants that live on or inside another animal or plant

species (SPEE-sheez) — one of the groups into which animals and plants of the same genus are divided

transparent (trans-PAIR-uhnt) — clear, like glass

Index

Page numbers in **bold** indicate illustrations.

About the Author

Vicky Franchino was very surprised to learn that chameleons do not change color to blend in with their surroundings! (Who knew?) She enjoyed doing research about the many ways that animals camouflage themselves. When Vicky told her daughter about the peppered moth and how it has changed color over time, she was very excited that her daughter remembered learning about this in biology class! Vicky lives with her family in Madison, Wisconsin.

Photo by Kat Franchino